LIVING on the
GROWING EDGE

LIVING on the GROWING EDGE

BY BRUCE LARSON

*A resource book for restless
and adventurous groups and individuals*

ZONDERVAN PUBLISHING HOUSE
Grand Rapids, Michigan

To *Christine*, *Peter*, and *Mark*
with whom I keep discovering 'the growing edge'

Introduction

WRITING THIS BOOK has been a great experience, for it has evolved out of preaching and teaching situations in a great number of churches, conferences, and groups all across the United States, Canada, and England.

Living on the Growing Edge deals with a variety of problems about which people are concerned, but it is not by any means a definitive or complete list of questions crucial to today's men and women. Rather, it merely suggests new approaches to ways in which God is helping people to grow and to understand Him and themselves and to receive His help.

As Christians we believe that Jesus Christ is the Great Physician. Even though medical knowledge keeps expanding all the time, it in no way minimizes Christ as the Healer through the ages. He is the Eternal Healer, but our understanding of the medical and spiritual resources for healing keeps growing. Thus we see in this an ever-expanding experience of God's concern for the whole man, and this book simply suggests new insights and new resources which may help us become whole people. It is an attempt to stimulate the kind of dialogue in which we may find our "growing edge" today.

The questions at the end of each chapter have been used mostly in small groups and workshops. The response to the ideas expressed and the results achieved from using questions have encouraged me to prepare such a book. I hope that many readers will use it and the questions as a springboard from which to go on to experiment and improvise.

Individuals may use them to examine their own lives in terms of past experience, present directions, and future goals. But the questions will be used most profitably by small groups of seekers who wish to discover God, the world, and themselves in new ways.

Groups using the questions should understand that no one will truly examine his own life or reveal himself to another unless he *wants* to. The questions will not pry self-revelation out of reluctant people, but they will be an aid for groups and individuals eager for adventure in spiritual depth and breadth.

The questions are not intended to be a study guide for the accompanying chapter. Rather, they are a supplementary resource for the general topic of the chapter, calling the group or the individual reader to further exploration. For that matter, a group could use only the questions in the book and omit the text completely and still enjoy a fascinating time of discovery.

Some sets of questions may be too long for a group to use at a single meeting. Either a selection of the best questions for that group will have to be made, or perhaps two meetings devoted to the topic. All in all, readers are urged to be flexible in the use of all the material presented here. It is a resource book that needs adapting.

Special thanks go to my wife Hazel and to Richard Engquist for much editorial help in the preparation of this book, and to Tekla Casperson who did most of the typing. Bertha Elliott has been of great help as both proofreader and editor. I'm deeply grateful to my good friends Geoff and Betty Kitson for the use of their home in Bermuda during the final stages of preparing the manuscript. And finally it must be said that this book could not have been written apart from God's gift of a great many spiritual adventurers who are partners in mission.

BRUCE LARSON

New York City

Table of Contents

LIVING on the
GROWING EDGE

1 | Living on the Growing Edge

"I KNOW THAT RENEWAL will have come to my church," said a friend of mine, the pastor of a suburban church in New Jersey, "when all the faithful people in the weekly prayer groups begin to be concerned about the plight of their neighbors in Newark, ten miles away, and when the men of my church who are deeply concerned about the internal affairs of Newark and involved in them begin to pray on a regular basis with one another."

My friend's concern for renewal is a concern which is voiced everywhere, in high and low churches, conservative and liberal. There is nothing new about renewal. God has always been calling His people to renewal from Old Testament times up to the present. What is important is that we understand the issues and imperatives of renewal for our time.

The suburban pastor's diagnosis of the need for renewal in his parish seems to pinpoint one of the major issues in the Western Church today. As Kagawa, the great Japanese Christian, said, "The trouble with America is that all your angels live in compartments."

The Church, like some business organizations, has been guilty of over-specialization. Some churches are known only for their emphasis on the individual's finding a right relationship to God through Jesus Christ. Others are preoccupied with self-acceptance or self-realization. Still others are concerned with creating healthy relationships between individuals in families, schools, offices, and neighborhoods. A fourth group is engaged in changing a world that has far too many citizens who are denied political freedom, financial security, social equality, or medical attention. Kagawa, during the years of his remarkable ministry in Japan, never "specialized," but worked in all four dimensions. He was an evangelist above all, but he lived in the slums and had a great concern for the social, economic, and moral betterment of his people.

Years ago someone observed that the Kingdom of God is the kingdom of right relationships. Jesus Christ said that the Kingdom of God is at hand. In other words, it is a present reality which ought to be observable in terms of right relationships. Above all, Christ came to make possible a right relationship between God and individuals. But He also came to make possible right relationships between individuals. He was further concerned about making right the relationship to oneself so that the person who cannot tolerate himself or who is a divided person can be reconciled to himself and accept himself because God loves him. Finally, Christ came to establish a right relationship between His followers and the world in which they live. He loved the world and established His Church to love the world in His name and by His Spirit. Renewal, for individuals or for a parish, hinges on the discovery of these four areas of right relationships that make up life as God intends us to live it.

Many congregations and individual Christians have become specialists in one or two of these relationships, but have ignored the others. People usually join churches that emphasize their own strengths and interests and reinforce their prejudices or blind spots. Authoritarian people affiliate with churches that confirm them in their opinions. Rebellious people seek churches that make no demands on their ethical or moral life. We go to a church that caters to our personal preferences, which stresses the relationship and dimension that is uppermost in our thoughts.

Renewal begins when a person is exposed to the forces that will stretch him and help him to discover the power of Christ in the relationships where he feels least secure. A church discovers renewal when it preaches and acts in a way which motivates the members to move from their own specialties into other dimensions of life.

The four right relationships mentioned above might be more recognizable in these terms: pietism, personalism, psychology or mental health, and social action. We all know particular parishes which have one of these labels — often to the exclusion of the other three. Each of these four concerns is valid and inherent in the

Gospel, and all four are stressed in the New Testament. The gospels and the letters of the New Testament affirm the primary need for a man to become right with God by accepting His unconditioned love in Jesus Christ, the gift of salvation in Him, and then attempting to live in costly obedience. There is also a constant stress on relationships between individuals. Jesus said, "If you bring your gift before the altar and have something against your brother, go to him and make the relationship right before you bring your gift to God." "We cannot love God whom we have not seen if we cannot love our brother whom we have seen." And the importance of self-acceptance is emphasized by Jesus' command to "love your neighbor as you love yourself," indicating that we must discover how to love ourselves when we are guilty and have missed the mark.

True self-acceptance begins at the cross as God's love is offered to us while we are rebellious and wrong. From the Christian perspective, this kind of self-acceptance is the beginning of integration for the individual. But Jesus is also concerned about the condition of people in the world about us. When John the Baptist sent his disciples to find out if Jesus were truly the Messiah, Jesus listed credentials entirely in terms of physical and social action: "Tell John that the lame walk, the blind see, the lepers are cleansed, and that the poor have good news preached to them."

The breeze of God's Spirit is blowing through the Church today as many are discovering the weakness of taking one dimension of the Gospel — or possibly two — and making it the whole Gospel. As the New Jersey pastor, quoted earlier, rightly observed, renewal comes for the Church when its members begin to enter into right relationships at all *four* basic levels.

Early in my ministry I met a remarkable teacher, one of those gifted people who realize that they are not teaching subjects but persons. In her classroom young people not only mastered learning skills, but began to understand themselves and life. This teacher was able consistently to encourage her students and help them to excel.

I asked this teacher what her method was. Her reply delighted me and enabled me to discover a concept common in education, but new to me, which changed my life and ministry and my understanding of God. She said that it is necessary to be aware of the "growing edge" of each student. The growing edge, it seems, is that area in the student's life where he is ready and able to learn. If you feed him material that he is intellectually or emotionally unable to handle, he is threatened and cannot learn. On the other hand, if you keep repeating things he has mastered, he becomes bored. A good teacher, my friend went on to say, must know what a student *needs* to learn and *is ready* to learn, and then present him with that material.

Surely this is how the Holy Spirit wants to work in each of our lives. Every one of us has a spiritual growing edge. We all have mastered certain skills and subjects and disciplines and formed certain attitudes. Our tendency is to sit back and make these the sum and substance of the Christian experience. On the other hand, God says, "Well done," and then moves us on to new areas that we can grasp and master. He urges us toward a total ministry.

When we are open to God's leading, we find that He pushes us into those relationships that threaten us most and in which we feel least comfortable. The Christian life is a dynamic in which no one can say,

"I have arrived." Rather, we have begun a life of commitment to Christ in which we find God prompting us to grow and learn and master new skills and establish new relationships.

Those who are living on the growing edge with God are open to hearing and experiencing things that may seem strange and "unorthodox." At the very point where we dull our growing edge and content ourselves with those things which we have already mastered, spiritual death begins to creep up on us. We all have a tendency to stand still and polish the past. We're like little children who love to have the same familiar stories read to them. They can almost repeat the stories from memory, yet it makes them feel secure and comfortable to hear the words repeated over and over again.

In the same way, people love to attend a church where they hear stressed those dimensions of the Gospel that they know and understand, and to which they can wholeheartedly shout "Amen!" God's renewal demands that churches with a pietistic emphasis begin to hear about the need for social action. Churches involved in social action need to hear about the need for finding a right relationship to God that begins to make a man whole and alive. Our maturity is seen in our ability to accept a threatening truth that someone else may bring to us about the amazing Gospel of Jesus Christ.

This is why renewal looks different for every church and every individual. The growing edge for each church and person *is* different. Let me describe two churches I know which are undergoing costly renewal. In each case fresh winds of the Spirit are blowing, not only through the immediate congregation but through the community as well.

The first is a wealthy old downtown church in a state capital city. For decades this church was known as a "Bible-centered church" where the Gospel was unashamedly preached and decisions called for each Sunday. In recent years, under an inspired pastor and staff, this church has added many new dimensions without abandoning its primary emphasis. Jesus Christ is still proclaimed as the Lord and Saviour of individuals. But the church has also begun to demonstrate an incarnate love for the people of the town, regardless of any personal response they may make to the Gospel. It has begun a day-care center for children of working mothers, and has initiated a ministry to nurses who live nearby. Members of the church are developing a concern for the many teen-age delinquents in that part of the city, a concern for the political life in that state capital, and a concern for the decisions made in its business life.

Renewal has not come by minimizing the former emphasis but by adding entirely new dimensions to this church's obedience to a radical Gospel.

The second church is located in an industrial town. For at least ten years this parish has been a bastion of social welfare, proclaiming that to follow God means to take responsibility in the affairs of labor and management, to fight for racial equality, and to care for the poor and for those living in ghettos. More recently, without minimizing its concern for the needs of people and for corporate decisions, this church has begun to form small groups in which people can discover a living Christ in depth relationships with one another. People are moving from a one-sided concern into total involvement with God, themselves, one another, and the town and world in which they live.

In both churches, as the growing edge is discovered, there is grumbling in the ranks. But the same Christ is at work illuminating the radically different areas of obedience necessary in these two cases.

Let me suggest what renewal might look like for two different Christian men. One is a son of privilege, educated in an Ivy-League college. He became a Christian many years ago. He knows the Bible backward and forward. He is concerned about his own soul and about the souls of others. He is a lay apostle and an evangelist in his own right. But he is so opposed to any kind of social action that a move by the town council to fluoridate the water supply would be viewed by him as a Communist plot. Renewal will come for this man as he moves from his tremendous concern for a right relationship between individuals and God into a concern for the society in which men live and which shapes their destinies.

The second man is a prophet in the area of social action. He has written a great deal and spoken all across the land, leading the Church in its growing concern for justice in every quarter of the economic, social, racial, and political arena. But this fearless servant of Jesus Christ is not only anti-pious, he is anti-personal. He hates small groups and any personal references in the pulpit. For him, the Gospel is solely concerned with healing the sick and preaching good news to the poor. Renewal can come to this man when he discovers the personal dimensions of the Gospel and adds them to his present relevant concerns for man as a social being.

Renewal in our time has to do with the discovery of the growing edge. The discovery is a personal thing for each individual, as it is a particular thing for each church. This is why we have seen the emergence of small groups. In small groups, people can examine their lives with a few others and discover how and where God wants them to grow. But there is no magic in small groups. They can be as ingrown or lopsided as any local church, emphasizing only Bible study *or* prayer *or* sensitivity training in mental health *or* action on social concerns. At its best, however, a small group is a place where individuals discover their strengths, and then move on to find what is necessary to their growth.

The small group ought to be made up of a number of individuals meeting regularly who know of the growing edge in each other's lives. In Bible study, honest fellowship, and prayer together, they can ask what God is calling each of them to do and encourage, affirm, and support each other in being and doing just that. The group should be a place where individuals begin to move into all four dimensions of right relationships.

I know a couple who are moving through the complete progression of right relationships. Neighbors in their apartment house invited them to attend a small group. At the first meeting they found people who cared for one another, who cared for them, who believed that Jesus Christ is alive and can change lives, and who were having fun. This typical young couple felt secure enough that first evening to confess the shaky condition of their own marriage and some personal problems with their children. They began their "pilgrims' progress" by moving into right relationship with a few other people week by week. Soon they could admit that they needed a right relationship to God through Jesus Christ. They were full of guilt, past and present, and they felt unloved. Individuals in the group helped them to turn their lives over to God and to accept His love for them. Thus a second dimension opened.

With this new-found freedom and forgiveness, they were able to examine themselves and to see some of the forces in their childhood that had contributed to present personality problems. Self-discovery and self-acceptance came gradually as they met with the group month after month. By the end of the first year, the husband, an engineer, discovered that faith in God was relevant to his work and to the people and the policies where he earned his livelihood. Amazing things happened as a result of his prayer and concern for people and situations at work. In the same way, his wife discovered her neighborhood as her natural mission field.

About a year ago at a pastors' conference, I was having lunch with six other men. Suddenly one young pastor leaned across the table and asked, "Bruce, do you find that you are becoming better as a Christian?"

At first I said, "Oh, yes!" Then, a moment later, "Well, no. . . . This is really a very difficult question, let me think for a moment."

Finally I told this new friend that while I supposed I was getting better, I certainly was more aware now of areas of disobedience in my life. Also, I had a much greater sense of failure. But I went on to say that the real issue for me was not in being better or worse, but rather in becoming the person God meant me to be.

I am growing in some of the right relationships already mentioned in a way that I would never have dreamed possible a few years ago. God is moving me from my securities into my insecurities, and I am meeting Him on the growing edge.

QUESTIONS FOR DISCUSSION

1. If the Kingdom of God is here *and* is the "Kingdom of Right Relationships" (to God, to self, to others, to the world), in which of the four relationships do you feel you *most* need to grow?

2. Give an example of your need from a recent experience.

3. If you belong to a church, what do you think its "growing edge" is in terms of helping its members discover the "Kingdom of Right Relationships"? Where is it most concerned and helpful? Where is it least concerned and helpful?

4. How do you feel you could enlarge the "growing edge" of your church's concern?

2 | A New Look at Marriage

A HOLIDAY TRADITION has grown in the family of a good friend of mine. Each Christmas, one of the gifts he receives from his wife is a large, intricate jigsaw puzzle. And each year the whole family works together during the holiday season to conquer this challenge. To add to the complication and the surprise, the wife always removes the picture from the cover of the box so that there will be no clue to what the finished puzzle will look like.

But last year she left the cover intact. The pieces of the puzzle were spread out over several tables and the work began. Days later, my friend and his children realized that the pieces they were working on would never make the picture on the box. His wife had bought two puzzles and switched the boxes.

This is a parable demonstrating much of the problem of planning for marriage. We have been given a false picture of what marriage should look like. Through well-meaning friends or teachers or preachers or through romantic literature we have an idealized picture of a truly Christian marriage.

Often, after years of trying to make the emotional, psychological, spiritual, and physical pieces fit together, we either give up and feel that our marriage is hopeless, or we discover that the picture God intends to show us is quite different and really much more fulfilling than the stereotype we had in mind.

It is important that a man and woman preparing for marriage understand something of the end product that God intends. If they look for a relationship without conflict, moodiness, or touchiness, with never any shadows to mar the light, they are bound to end in frustration and despair. But if they see that God calls people together into a relationship where they can learn true communication, both verbal and non-verbal, and in which there can be genuine appreciation and affirmation, enjoyment of each other as persons, and the thrill of working toward shared goals, then it is easy to accept the humanness that each brings to marriage and which produces honest conflict.

Each of us tends to look for a spouse who is "Mr. Right" or "Miss Right." We all know people who have reached middle age still unmarried, though they have had opportunities. When we get to know such people well, we often find that they have been looking for the wrong Mr. Right or Miss Right.

One friend told me she almost didn't marry the man who is now her husband because she was a college graduate and he used bad grammar. In her mind's eye, she had a very real picture of Mr. Right, but she almost missed him when he came along. Happily, she belonged to a small group fellowship, and God used her friends to give her the correction she needed.

Instead of looking for the "right" person, we should look for the "guided" person. God, in His love, often sends to us people who do not fit our preconceived notions of what a spouse should look like, and we need to be alert to the kind of relationship God wants for us if we are to discover *His* choice.

The person who fits our preconceptions and seems almost too good to be true may be the worst possible choice, while the one who does not measure up in any way at first sight may be just the one God has in mind for us. Let me give two illustrations:

One couple of my acquaintance have endured years of a most unfruitful marriage. I sense in their relationship a quiet desperation. They are from the same town, the same social set, and the same church. Both are quiet, respectable people, neither very communicative nor argumentative. There is nothing wrong with their marriage, but there is nothing right with it, either. They are simply living on the fringes of fulfillment and adventure and involvement. They have each other, but that doesn't seem to be enough.

I think of another couple, recently married, who have totally dissimilar backgrounds. The girl is from a rural area, the man from the heart of a great city. He never finished high school; she has a master's degree. He comes from a broken home, and she from a secure and happy family.

There is almost nothing these two have in common except a great desire to know and serve God and a great joy in being part of each other. Already they have been a blessing to all who know them, and some of us who have been married for years are learning from them much of what God intends for a Christian marriage.

Let me suggest some guidelines that may be helpful as you choose a spouse. These characteristics may be of some value as you seek to find the "guided" person, rather than some nonexistent Mr. or Miss Right.

(1) *Complementary personalities.* There is much wisdom in the old saying that opposites attract. If we are free of the wrong kinds of preconceptions, we tend to be drawn to those who are really quite different in traits, gifts, and personalities. It is as if God is putting dissimilar people together so that they can help each other in their limitations and needs. Two halves come together to make a whole person.

To be more specific, savers should marry spenders; talkers should marry listeners; gregarious people should marry home-lovers; the sensual should marry the esthetic; the adventurous should marry the cautious; those who are thought-motivated should marry those who are motivated more by feeling and instinct.

By contrast, imagine what happens when you marry someone like yourself. It must be hell on earth for two compulsive talkers to be married to each other! Two savers can miss out on much that is good in life, and two spenders can end up in bankruptcy. In making plans, there is much to be said for instinct, but thought and preparation should certainly go into every decision. How marvelous it is when each half of a marriage complements the other.

(2) *Similar goals.* Though it may be quite right for people of contrasting personality to marry, it must be said that the real basis for a Christian marriage is having similar or even identical goals. By goals I mean what it is you want to do with your life and how you want to spend the resources of time, talent, and energy that God has given you. The ideal couple is one that, though possibly very different in personality, desires to use the resources of life to attain the same goals.

When two Christians marry they should both want to serve God and others with their lives and talents. It is tragic when one is committed and oriented in this way, but married to someone who really wants some form of success, wealth, fame, or security. There is at the heart of such a marriage a great rift that is never healed until both partners discover God and a true motivation for life.

Where goals are different, there is constant hostility, competition, and in-fighting. It's difficult enough to live together where there are identical goals!

(3) *Enjoyment of sex.* Although it is true that a satisfying sex life does not by itself make a good marriage, it is difficult to imagine a happy marriage without a satisfying sex life. God made sex to be enjoyed mutually by married couples. When one of the partners has emotional or psychological problems that prevent this, there is a barrier in the marriage.

We need to understand that purity outside the marital union does not mean a repressive attitude toward sex within the marriage bond. When God makes a man and woman free and whole by the gift of His Spirit, one sign of wholeness is certainly the sacramental enjoyment of sex.

Whenever I talk to young people about courtship, I always caution them to be careful about a fiance who seems to have no interest in physical love. The healthiest kind of relationship between two Christians who intend to marry is one, I believe, where both are strongly drawn to each other sexually but in which both understand that premarital sexual intercourse would destroy something wonderful and sacred that God has planned, and each helps the other to abstain. Lack of interest in physical love, which often passes for sexual purity, may actually signal a difficult psychological maladjustment — for example, latent homosexuality.

(4) *Friendship.* The greatest compliment, to me, that you can pay your spouse is to say that he is your best friend. A man and woman are truly happy if they enjoy being alone together, talking, laughing, discussing, philosophizing, dreaming, and praying. This is friendship at its highest level.

The couple that is over-focused on sex is missing out on the best part of marriage. But, of course, friendship alone is not enough, nor does it warrant marriage. Both sex and friendship are a part of what God has planned for the marital relationship.

Several years ago at a midnight bull-session in the dormitory of an Ivy-League college, a young man spoke up — and I suspect he spoke for a number of the men there. "I feel I owe it to my wife to have premarital sex experience," he said.

Nothing could be more unrealistic. Premarital sex is never good preparation for marriage, even if it is with the person you intend to wed. The greatest gift we can bring to a marriage partner is amateur status. Marriage is the fun of learning together how to communicate physically, spiritually, and emotionally.

But behind that young man's words I heard him expressing a desire for premarital *openness*. The best preparation I know for marriage is to begin to talk deeply about who you are, how you understand yourself, what you want in life, what you are afraid of, and all the rest that makes you a unique individual. This kind of openness can pave the way for understanding in marriage. Marriage should simply be the continuation of that kind of open relationship where discovery of each other and of oneself is constantly taking place. Depth discovery should begin before marriage, or chances are it will not take place after the wedding.

It is sad when we embark on marriage as two strangers. We are then caught in a terrible trap like that of a young woman who once said to me, "I'm going to be married in a few weeks. I can't wait to get married so I can start to be myself again."

If we have to play a role in order to win someone's love, then we are forced to continue playing that role for the rest of our lives — or risk letting the person know what we are really like and possibly losing his love!

That is why I believe premarital openness is the best preparation for marriage, and the door two people walk through to one of life's most exciting adventures.

QUESTIONS FOR DISCUSSION

1. Describe a couple you know who you feel have a truly happy marriage.

2. What do you think makes their marriage satisfying for both?

3. What relationship (if any) do you think this couple have to Jesus Christ?

4. Describe what you think the "ideal" mate would be like.

5. Describe your long-range goals for marriage, whether you are now married or hope to be married.

3 | A New Look
at the Family

WHEN OUR SON's Sunday school teacher asked the class of four-year-olds who God was, his hand went up. "God is a great big Presbyterian minister," he said.

While his response caused a good many chuckles in our congregation, it is not really an unusual one. Most young children have a hard time differentiating between God and their parents. This realization is enough to frighten the wits out of any conscientious Christian parent. Who, by his actions, wants to be responsible for God's character and reputation in the eyes of his children?

Since that time a quiet revolution has taken place

in our home. Our daughter and our two sons are now able to distinguish between God and their parents. This has completely changed our family devotions, the children's prayers, and all of our life together. Spiritually, our family has become three dimensional: children, parents, and the Living Christ.

Very simply, my wife and I have stopped being our children's priests who plan family worship, hear their prayers and confessions, and pray for their well-being. We still do these things, but we also confess our sins to God in the presence of our children and, with them, receive His forgiveness.

You can see immediately what happens. God is no longer someone in league with harassed parents, used by them to keep children in line. He is not the property of parents, a kind of grown-up secret, like Santa Claus. Rather, He is God of both parent and child, a very real person before whom each member of the family must kneel.

If I were to say that this "revolution" had not cost me a great deal in the way of pride, I would not be telling the truth. And, in spite of the fact that "losing face" is a small price to pay for a new and deeper relationship to my children and our deeper relationship to God, I am still constantly tempted by pride to "save face" and play priest when trouble arises in which I am involved.

Perhaps an illustration will demonstrate this new dimension in our family. When the children were smaller, I had spent most of one Saturday playing with them. Since I had been away from home for several days and was about to leave for another week, it seemed only right that they should have Father all to themselves for one day.

We rough-housed, drove in the country, and bought a book about parakeets in the dime store. I promised to begin reading the new book to them that night just before they went to bed.

Church business after dinner kept me away longer than I had planned, and when I returned home it was already a little past bedtime. The children, though, had managed to stay up until my return and eagerly met me at the door with book in hand.

Well, I walked into my home just as the first strains of the theme song from my favorite TV show were coming from the set in the den. Immediately my soul was the battleground for conflicting emotions. I wanted very much to be an exemplary father, to keep my promise to read the book, and so complete a "perfect day" with my children. At the same time, I was drowning in a wave of self-pity. Here I had spent a whole day being a good father. Were my children so selfish and inconsiderate as to demand the surrender of this one cherished hour held sacred each week? Legally they had me. I had promised. But morally I was certain no jury would convict me for breaking my promise under the circumstances.

With rising voice and flushed face (I never was good at concealing guilt) I tried to make my children see how unreasonable they were. My daughter knew better than to argue back. She merely let two big tears spill from her eyes and run down her cheeks. Thus pierced by a sharper sword than law or logic, I demanded the book and said (between clenched teeth) that I *would* read to them. My daughter then protested and begged me to watch my favorite show. But I insisted on reading. (If one has demonstrated himself a fool, he may as well be a martyr!) That is, I insisted until my wife sternly intervened and told me (in no uncertain terms) to watch TV; that she would read to the children.

I have seldom spent a more miserable hour. When the show was over, my wife said she wanted to speak to me. I was sure she did, but what she had to say surprised me. She said we had come to a place where the selfishness of any individual member of the family was no shock to the other members. What did concern her, however, was my own refusal to let others in the family repent when they truly wanted to. In the case under discussion, both my daughter and I were wrong. But when she really wanted to back down and change the situation, my own guilt would not permit it.

My wife's words burned home. I was no longer ashamed of only a single incident, but of a whole attitude. I quietly prayed and asked Christ to forgive me and to change me. Immediately as I felt His healing begin and His love at work, I wanted to share this with my daughter and to ask her forgiveness.

I found her pretending to be asleep when I whispered her name. Finally she sat up and heard my confession, only to interrupt it with her own. After we both laughingly insisted "It was my fault" many times, she wisely informed me that it was just because we are the kind of people we are that Christ came into the world to love us and forgive us. She was neither shocked nor upset by my recent infantile behavior, but suggested that we pray, both of us, and ask forgiveness. After our prayers, we both felt each other's love more deeply and thanked God for His love that once again made it possible for us to love each other without guilt or resentment.

It costs a great deal for a parent to worship God with a broken and a contrite heart in the presence of his children, but I thank God that He has helped me to begin. I wouldn't live any other way.

While this incident reveals my own "growing edge," I think it should be said that some parents don't need to be broken, but rather need to be starched and strengthened.

A few weeks before I started writing this chapter I had lunch with a businessman from Texas, whom I'll call George. "What is the most exciting thing that God is doing in your life now?" I asked him, knowing that he had begun the Christian life some five or six years ago.

He pondered for a moment and then said, "I'm not sure I can explain it, or that you will understand or even appreciate it. The fact is, all my life I have been known as a 'good guy.' Everybody thought of me as 'good old George.' Even my family thought I was soft and easygoing.

"Well, since I have discovered the reality of Jesus Christ and God's love for me, I realize that much of my being a good guy has been weakness, and a desire to be loved because I was insecure. Now I find that Christ is giving me the freedom to lay down rules for my family and to back them up. And out in the world, I am free for the first time to object when someone pushes in front of me in a line. This is a new freedom for me, and I find it very exciting."

I told George I could appreciate what was happening to him, and suggested that this shows clearly that there is a unique shape of salvation for each of us. Jesus Christ saves us from all kinds of traps and pitfalls and wrong thinking about ourselves, and His salvation may look different for each one.

"What does your family think of you now that you are no longer a 'good guy'?" I asked George.

"It's the most amazing thing," he answered. "They all like the new me! I think my sense of authority, and the fact that I am taking spiritual and moral leadership in my home, has given them rules and structures that they have needed for growth and maturity. It has brought my wife and my children and me all closer together."

This incident, which is so very different from my own situation, shows the remarkable work that God is up to in each individual life and each family. The important thing is for us to understand what must be added or taken away from our lives so that we can love those entrusted to us with a more complete and liberating kind of love.

QUESTIONS FOR DISCUSSION

1. What qualities or traits do you most admire in your parents?

2. What qualities or traits do you find least desirable in your parents?

3. What qualities or traits do you want your family to appreciate most in you?

4. What are the characteristics of a family you know personally who seem most like what you think a Christian family ought to be?

5. Tell of specific instances in the life of that family where you have seen those characteristics at work.

6. What spiritual resources does that family have or use which account for their style of life as a family?

7. What specific steps or disciplines would your family need to take to make use of the same resources?

4 | A New Look at Love

DURING FAMILY WORSHIP some years ago, we were amazed to hear our five-year-old son begin his prayer by saying, "O Lord, don't be afraid of us!" When prayers were finished, it struck me that Mark had perceived clearly the true mystery of God's love as revealed in the coming of His Son. In the birth, life, and death of Jesus Christ, God has put Himself in the position where we — His creatures — can hurt Him, the Creator. This is the scandal of the Incarnation. It seems a contradiction for the creature to have the power to inflict wounds on the Creator.

Stripping away all the sentiment that has built up

over the centuries about a beautiful December night in Bethlehem, a quaint inn, a lovely young mother, and a worried husband, we discover that God sent His Son to be born in a dirty stable, to parents who would shortly be fleeing for their lives. God became so involved in the world that He was vulnerable.

For many years after I became a Christian, the God described in John 3:16, "For God so loved the world that He gave His only begotten Son. . ." was incomprehensible to me. Having come through World War II, I could understand a man giving his life for others and, on occasion, I saw some heroic examples of this. But I had difficulty understanding a Father who sacrificed His Son to make atonement for the sins of mankind.

Only now that I am a father can I understand the vicarious suffering of a parent. How many times have I stood helplessly by and watched one of our children being ignored, abused, ridiculed, or humiliated? As children grow older, we see them victimized by insensitive teachers or ignored by their companions. The pain of these situations is a hundred times greater than it was when years ago I suffered through all of this myself. As a father I can appreciate in a very small measure the tremendous cost of God's love for us in allowing His only Son to become so involved with mankind that He was totally vulnerable, beginning with His birth in a stable and ending with His death upon the cross.

The Christian style of life can be summed up in two ideas: understanding the costly nature of God's love and then loving others in the same way He loves us. Jesus' great commandment to us is that we "love one another as I have loved you."

Frequently I find myself living provisionally. I hold back for fear of being hurt. I am reminded of my first agonizing years of playing football at school. Afraid of being hurt, I was reluctant to play the game with all my might. Consequently, by playing provisional football and holding back, I took a terrific beating.

What the coaches had been trying to tell us finally got through. The more you try to protect yourself, the more you will be hurt. When you give the game everything you've got, you are in much less danger of receiving injuries. The Christian life is like that, too. As we willingly lose our lives, we find that we actually save them and begin to be relevant to the world's needs in the name of Christ.

A long-time missionary to India, now in very active retirement, gave me this poem entitled "The Devil's Lie":

> They say that a man must live.
> Who says that a man must live?
> That is the devil's lie.
> Sometimes it happens that a man must die.

William Stringfellow, a young New York lawyer, spent the first years of his practice living in a tenement in East Harlem. He has written these words: "To become and to be a Christian is, therefore, to have the extraordinary freedom to share the burdens of the daily, common, ambiguous, transient, perishing existence of men, even to the point of actually taking the place of another man, whether he be powerful or weak, in health or in sickness, clothed or naked, educated or illiterate, secure or persecuted, complacent or despondent, proud or forgotten, housed or homeless, fed or hungry, at liberty or in prison, young or old, white or Negro, rich or poor."*

The dynamic in the life of so many effective Christians I've known has to do with this kind of involvement and vulnerability. To live like this is difficult and it requires all the power that God can give to His people as they seek to be obedient in specific situations.

One of the problems in marriage is that neither partner dares to become truly vulnerable to the other. I know a couple, active in their church and raising three fine children. They had no serious problems on the surface, but their relationship throughout the first years of their married life was superficial. The turning point came when the wife, after much spiritual searching, dared to tell her husband what kind of person she had been before she married him, and of the phoniness and pretense in her life after they were married. When he had recovered from the initial hurt and shock, the husband made the same kind of response. To begin truly to know each other was costly and painful, but they are finding a new relationship and a new love for each other, and God is beginning to make them a source of healing to many people.

A contemporary theologian points up the spiritual truth discovered by this couple in these words: "Man is a sinner. That is his condition. When man pretends he is not a sinner, that is sin." Sin is anything that separates us from one another and from God. Therefore, it is not our acts that are the source of sin, but our pretense of being better or different than we are.

---

*From *My People Is the Enemy*, by William Stringfellow. Copyright © 1964. Used by permission of Holt, Rinehart and Winston, Inc.

When someone dares to break out of the trap of un-
reality in a marriage or family situation, he usually discovers a new dimension in every other relationship.

Those who are members of Alcoholics Anonymous
are involved in a ministry to one another and are
totally vulnerable because of their honesty about past
failures and present needs. This has produced a chain
reaction of changed and liberated lives.

A business executive who is an active leader in AA
recently gave me this description of the four paradoxes
of AA: (1) We surrender to win. (2) We must give
away to keep. (3) We have to suffer to get well. (4)
We have to die to live.

Perhaps something should be said at this point about
the interrelatedness of strength and weakness. God
urges us in the Scriptures to "be strong." "Be strong in
the Lord" is something we have all heard over and over
again as a valid Christian exhortation. But many of us
have confused strength with weakness. The thing that
often drives a person to drink is his rigidity and im-
mobility in relationships. He cannot admit he is wrong,
and refuses to take any kind of correction or criticism.
Because he tries to be strong in the wrong way, he is
driven — through his own particular weakness — to an
escape which is real weakness.

What appears to be weakness in a member of Alcoholics Anonymous is actually a new kind of strength.
He can now take correction and criticism, and he can
admit that he is wrong. And he can examine his own
life critically in the fellowship of AA and in his own
personal inventory. He no longer has to look strong to
the world, and therefore he finds a new kind of strength.
Certainly this reminds us of our Lord Himself, whose
strength was demonstrated perhaps most magnificently

in His trial and crucifixion. Though He had defended the innocent in the temple, He did not defend Himself, and He was able to absorb the lies hurled against Him by His accusers.

This new kind of strength that looks like weakness can have a tremendous effect on those around us when we discover it by God's grace. A woman I know who has begun to live her life under new management tells about a recent change in her relationship to her husband. For years she had been the "strong Christian" in the family, urging her husband to do his duty in all kinds of ways, and making most of the family decisions including how much to contribute to the church and to various charitable causes.

Through a profound spiritual experience, she realized that her strong, almost dictatorial attitude was incompatible with God's will for her. She determined to try to make her husband happy, instead of trying to make him "good."

Not long afterward, there was a fund drive in their church, and her husband asked how much they should contribute. This time she did not suggest an amount, but left the decision to him, pretending that she did not really care. She was staggered to discover that he had written a check for five times the amount she would have suggested and fought for. It is in this kind of "weakness" that we discover strength. It is a kind of strength that is communicated to others as we stop fighting with them and defer to them.

At the first Faith at Work conference in England I met a delightful little woman, frail and delicate looking. Her story, as I heard it from friends who had known her for years, was astonishing. She was the first white woman born in Kenya. Her parents were missionaries and her formative years were spent in the mission fields of Africa. In middle age she returned to Dublin with her sister. One night during a prayer meeting, while she was earnestly seeking God's will for her life, she sensed that He was telling her to care for homeless children in the streets of Dublin.

Clara got up off her knees, corralled a teammate, and the two of them went off at once to explore the city streets. That first night they prayed with a drunken man in the street who wanted to begin a new life, and they brought home a young wife who had left her husband. A work in Dublin was begun which has led to the rehabilitation of hundreds and hundreds of people, including criminals, orphans, strays, and drunks.

As God gave this little woman her marching orders, she immediately became involved and vulnerable. This seems to be His plan for each person who becomes obedient. A town can change when one person begins to love as God has loved him.

During my visit to England, a man with great faith and a humble spirit shared his motto with me: "It's a great life if you weaken." This is the core of dynamic Christianity. God in His perfect strength became weak and vulnerable in the Incarnation, and He calls those who know and serve Him to do the same.

QUESTIONS FOR DISCUSSION

1. What kind of social gathering or party do you enjoy most?

2. Describe your favorite way of spending spare time.

3. Are you the kind of person others confide in?

4. What kind of person do you confide in?

5. What makes a person a good listener?

6. What kind of listener do you think you have been in this group?

7. How do you feel this group has listened to you?

5 | A New Look at Fear

Two VERY DIFFERENT men have taught me a great deal in years past about fear and how to handle it. One was a venerable and highly respected doctor; the other, a professional wrestler.

The doctor, a surgeon, confided that there were only two things in life that he feared — the loss of his skilled hands and a possible impairment of his breathing. Within two years he suffered a double attack: emphysema in his lungs and crippling arthritis in his hands!

Here we see one of the most mysterious and puzzling aspects of fear — its magnetism.

51

The teenager afraid of unpopularity will almost certainly be a wallflower. The businessman afraid of failure or bankruptcy is likely to have financial difficulty. A possessive mother afraid of losing her children's love and affection will probably experience rejection in painful ways. In the grip of fear, we seem to hasten the approach of the feared object or event.

On the positive side, there is a way to deal with fear that minimizes its power and its effect, and may even turn that fear into an advantage. This is where the wrestler can speak to us.

He stood a magnificent 6' 9" and was a new Christian, giving his witness with telling effect. When asked how he had happened to become a wrestler, he replied that all through his teen-age years he had been a tall, skinny boy with little strength and much fear of physical contact. Then he read a book from which these words jumped off the page: "Do the thing you fear most and the death of fear is certain." He saw the implication at once and began a body-building program that led to his joining a wrestling team.

The Viennese psychiatrist, Viktor Frankl, says, "The cue to cure is self-commitment." These wise words from the father of logotherapy echo a corresponding spiritual message from the Bible: Commit yourself to Christ and do the very thing you fear most.

I would suggest at least six steps to handle fear. Since scientific truth and authentic revelation are never in conflict, and since God is the author of both, we may draw freely from these two sources.

(1) *Analyze your fear.* There are at least two kinds of fear. One kind can be a good friend and a genuine gift of God, but the other is certainly a deadly enemy.

Let us label these "healthy fear" and "unhealthy fear."

Healthy fear keeps us from destroying ourselves or others physically, mentally, emotionally, and socially. Children learn fear early in life. They develop a healthy respect for busy streets, hot stoves, and sharp knives. As a small boy I was intrigued by a newfangled cigarette lighter in the car of a friend who came to visit. I was warned never to push it in or to touch it. Well, of course, at the first opportunity I did just that — and for weeks carried a painful circular brand on my thumb. I have been wary of cigarette lighters ever since!

In the adult world an active conscience which tells us when we are morally right or wrong can be a barometer of healthy fear. Fear of consequences often keeps a man honest, moral, true to his convictions, or responsible as a member of his group. A newly-emerging school of psychiatry is violently anti-Freudian and declares that a man's conscience is his best friend. It affirms "middle-class Victorian values" that keep a man from becoming a thief or a philanderer. Freud thought that a too-strict conscience caused mental breakdown. The new psychiatry says that mental breakdown comes because we do *not* listen to our conscience and enter into mental conflict as a result, and that when we begin to bring our performance up to acceptable standards, we find mental health.

Generally speaking, healthy fear is based on external threats which are real. To be afraid of real danger is certainly a healthy thing. Unhealthy fear, on the other hand, often appears in the form of anxiety, which springs from inner motivations that may or may not be grounded in reality. We are afraid of rejection, or we are afraid of our own worthlessness, or we are afraid of failing in any one of a thousand ways. This internal anxiety can make all the external aspects of life loom like grotesque giants. To be motivated by inner fears is spiritual myopia. We see life in a distorted way and react in panic.

This is the very opposite of living by faith, which begins when we see things as they really are. This does not eliminate healthy fears, but puts external forces in their true perspective.

So it helps to take an honest look at the things you fear most. Jot them down on a piece of paper and show it to a trusted friend or counselor. Try to discover whether these are healthy or unhealthy fears. Once you have done this, much of the problem may already be solved.

A woman of great faith visited her doctor for an examination. A few days later he told her that she had cancer and that her days were numbered. At first she panicked and fear took over. But in a few moments she regained her perspective and smilingly replied, "Well, *your* days are numbered too." She realized that the doctor had not introduced any new evidence. Ironically, the woman outlived her doctor by several years, though he was much younger than she. But the important thing was not her extended life span, but the fact that she lived her remaining years free from fear.

(2) *Pay attention to healthy fears.* Often we are in a panic because we are doing something we should not do or neglecting something we should do. This can be the basis for mental breakdown. The old Freudian psychiatry said that because people felt rejected or worthless or full of self-hatred, their per-

formance broke down. The theory was that when your feelings improved, your performance also improved. Clinical evidence seems to indicate that this theory has little validity.

But amazing breakthroughs are coming through the new psychiatry in terms of treatment and cure. Present-day pioneers of the mind such as Glasser, Szasz, Mowrer, and Parker say that feelings *follow* performance. A man *feels* worthless because he is *doing* poorly. This school of psychiatry tries to help a man perform better (to learn to love, to learn to be honest, to learn to be responsible), so that his feelings about himself will improve. This is certainly not unlike the Biblical message calling for repentance. When a man's life is changed, he finds that he feels better and that he may genuinely begin to love God and others and even himself.

(3) *Don't fight unhealthy fears.* Viktor Frankl stresses this in homely, simple terms. He says the more you fight an object you fear, the more you increase its hold on you. If you are troubled by insomnia, the worst thing to do is try to sleep. If you are a stutterer, the worst thing you can do is try not to stutter.

Frankl reports great success in helping people with such symptoms. He tells the insomniac to go to bed, saying that he is going to stay awake all night and possibly for many nights. When he makes a game of not sleeping and trying to stay awake, sleep usually comes sooner than expected.

This noted psychiatrist also tells about a bookkeeper who lost his job because his excellent handwriting became scribbling. The harder he tried to keep from scribbling, the worse his handwriting became. The doctor told the bookkeeper to begin to scribble as illegibly as he could. When he tried to scribble, he found that he could not, and his former handwriting returned.

Another case involved a boy with a stuttering problem, who discovered, when he tried to win sympathy by forcing himself to stutter, that he was unable to do so.

Praying to have our fear removed usually avails little. As Christians we should pray instead for courage to launch into action, in spite of our fears.

(4) *Learn to laugh at yourself.* When we take ourselves too seriously, we only aggravate our problems and become more difficult to live with. Gordon Allport has said, "The neurotic who learns to laugh at himself may be on the way to self-management, perhaps cure." This advice from a psychiatrist is profoundly Christian in its implications. The heart of the Christian message is that God loves us and accepts us in spite of recurring fear and failure. We should therefore be able to see ourselves with relaxation and good humor.

(5) *Risk failure.* In Biblical terms, live by faith! This is another way of suggesting that we do the very thing we fear most.

The story is told of a shipwreck off the New England coast many years ago. A young member of the Coast Guard rescue crew said, "We can't go out — we'll never get back!" The grizzled old captain replied, "We have to go out! We *don't* have to come back." This kind of living cuts the sinews of fear.

Christian security has little to do with success or failure. As Christians we believe that Christ loves us totally whether we succeed or fail. This gives us a new base from which to follow God in mission to the world. If we believe that God loves us regardless of our performance, we do not have to hide our failures from ourselves, from our fellowmen, or from God Himself. The important thing is that we try to find God's will and do it, and admit when we have missed the mark or failed.

Ultimately we never know whether we have succeeded. The cross looked like dismal defeat, but it was God's greatest triumph. It may even be said that the will of God for us is not that we accomplish an objective, but that we attempt it. In the case of America's war on poverty, for example, we believe it is God's will that we work toward the elimination of poverty, inequality, and ignorance. Whether this war will be wholly won is irrelevant. God does not hold us responsible for success, but for obedience. He will judge us by our efforts, not by our successes.

(6) *Recognize fear as faith in reverse.* Even unhealthy fear can be an asset to a Christian if it points out to him the focus of his spiritual needs and the particular requirements for faith. When you know your fears, you can almost certainly find God's challenge to you. Do the thing you fear and you find that you are acting in faith.

A few months ago I attended a great laymen's institute in the Midwest, sponsored by a large denomination. The members were talking about a radical change planned for next year's program. Many men who had been present at this convocation for years were in a panic. Over lunch I turned to one of the leaders and said, "How do you think next year's program will be?" He answered with a smile, "It will be just what we make it." Here we see faith at work. The same situation induced fear in some men and faith in others.

Christians should enjoy the freedom to fail. Many years ago I had to make a momentous decision about my career. For weeks I prayed that God would give me guidance, but no clarity came. During this time I urged my wife to pray for guidance and to confirm what I suspected was God's will.

One day she told me that she would gladly go wherever I went, but that she had no light on this next move. Then I realized that much of my desire for God's guidance was a fear of failure. I wanted my wife's confirmation in the move so that if it ended in failure, we would fail together.

New freedom came when I made the decision with dispatch, not knowing if it were right. My fear of failure in the situation was gone. I came to my new job with enthusiasm and with a great sense of God's love and presence. "Perfect love casts out fear!"

Living by faith does not mean that we will always be right, guided, or successful. Part of the Christian style of life involves a spontaneity in which we lose our fear of failure and move out in the light of the guidance that we have, acknowledging that we may be wrong. It is reassuring to read the book of Acts and find reports of failure among the first-century Christians. They set up a communal society that failed. They failed to believe in the power of prayer; when they prayed for Peter in prison and the angel let him out, they wouldn't let him in to their prayer meeting! They did not understand the unique thing God had initiated among the Gentiles, and for years refused to accept them as equals. For years they doubted Saul's conversion. They refused to obey the Lord's command to "go into all the world," and were driven by persecution to do so. They had to appoint deacons to preside at table because of in-fighting. Drunkenness, incest, laziness, jealousy, all were found among the Christians. The list of failures goes on and on.

They were far from perfect people, but they had a joy and a dependence on God. They did not hesitate to act for fear that they might be wrong. They believed that God could use even their errors if they were free to admit them and to change their ways.

True freedom in Christ is to enjoy the freedom to fail. This is God's answer to fear!

QUESTIONS FOR DISCUSSION

1. What or whom do you most trust in, other than God?

2. Whose approval do you need the most?

3. In whose presence are you most uncomfortable? Why?

4. What feelings do you have trouble expressing or controlling?

5. What circumstances tend to make you irritable or furious?

6. What circumstances tend to make you depressed or blue?

7. What circumstances tend to make you anxious, worried, or afraid?

8. What accomplishments have given you genuine self-respect?

9. List some creative ways to begin and end a day.

6 | A New Look at Commitment

WHEN AN ESTABLISHED Virginia businessman decided several years ago that Jesus Christ was calling him to the ordained ministry, a startled colleague exclaimed, "I didn't know business was *that* bad!"

Perhaps this is not an unusual reaction to the idea of a present-day call from God. Most of us accept the Biblical account of Christ's call to His first disciples, but it is more difficult to believe that Christ is alive in the world today and is calling men in the same way.

A conference was scheduled in a downtown hotel in Hamilton, Ontario, and on the marquee a huge sign read: "Welcome Faith at Work." Directly across the

61

street a theatre marquee advertised, in letters just as large, "Hell on Earth." Though amused by this graphic contrast, some of us were nevertheless made aware of an eternal option: we may put our faith to work in response to Christ's call, or we may live a hell on earth — an endless variety of hells of our own making.

There is a profound search today for *radical* or *root Christianity*. Bonhoeffer describes it as "religionless Christianity" which is authentic for any age, any group, any culture. It is always refreshing to realize that there is nothing intrinsically "religious" about the Gospel. Miraculously, the Gospel has flourished in the midst of a variety of religious expressions and cultural trappings. One can only applaud as the search goes on for the timeless Gospel behind religion, culture, and traditions.

Any serious search takes us back to the Scriptures. The first chapter of Mark's Gospel indicates at least three elements of an authentic call to discipleship.

I. *Commitment to a Person*

Christ's call to His first disciples was a person-to-person call. They were not called to believe a doctrine, practice an ethic, or worship in a prescribed way. Rather, they were called to trust Jesus and follow Him.

The original call was not to people who could be considered "spiritual types," those who naturally enjoy prayer, meditation, and the esthetics of worship. Instead, Jesus called men who were virile, earthy, and ordinary. We might have expected Him to call people with "time on their hands" — the rich, the unemployed, or the retired — but instead He called middle-class businessmen with vested interests. Certainly our Lord calls people with a spiritual bent, but He is no respecter of persons. Men and women from every walk of life who are willing to respond are called.

How odd, too, that no time limit was implied in that original call. Jesus merely asked four fishermen to follow Him. Did they interpret this as an invitation for that day, or for a week, or possibly for several years? When they left their businesses, their friends, their familiar surroundings, and even their families to follow Jesus Christ, they could not have known it was to be a lifetime call.

A certain layman has been one of the pioneers in land reapportionment in the world's underdeveloped areas, working for the United Nations and for private foundations. His leadership has changed the conditions of thousands, and he has personally introduced scores of people to a living Christ.

He tells an almost incredible story of his original call. Intrigued by a group of Christians and dissatisfied with much of his own life, he was at first frightened by the totality of Christian commitment. One of his new friends asked if he would consider turning his life over to Christ's management for a one-week trial.

"That's too long," was his reply.

"How about one day?"

"Can't do it."

"How about one hour?"

Hesitatingly, he said yes. You can guess the rest. Since that moment he hasn't lived life on the old terms.

According to Mark, Jesus extracted no promise to be "good" from His first disciples. Yet I am sure they eventually found themselves practicing a quality of life that would have seemed impossible when they first responded.

Recently *The New York Times* carried an interview with the pastor of a Protestant parish in Prague, Czechoslovakia. He said, "In the past, people came to church for many reasons. Some came to worship; others came to be seen. It was the thing to do, you understand. Now it is no longer the thing to do. Today there is only one reason to come to church, and that is because you have faith."

The pastor admitted that he preaches to smaller congregations nowadays, but he added that there is an intensity and seriousness, especially among the young, that formerly was missing. He said that within the hour he would be meeting with a Bible study group of young adults who fit this description. "They do not spare the Church," he reported. "They tell me that the traditional service is meaningless to modern man, that my sermons belong to another age. They remind me regularly that the past is gone forever. But I have never known such Christians! There are about forty of them. They are not the kind of Christians I grew up with. They take it all very seriously. Most of us did not."

Karl Barth has called religion a sin. What he implies is that Christianity is not *a religion* but *an encounter between a living Christ and living men.* Christianity is not the greatest of the religions, but rather an encounter between The Person and any person who hears His call and responds. We respond to Christ's call not with "true" or "false" but with "yes" or "no!"

II.   *Commitment to Life Together*

The authentic Christian call described by Mark is also a call to life in fellowship with other people. Many of

Jesus' first followers were called in two's — Simon and Andrew, James and John — and very soon the two's became twelve. Often the Church has emphasized commitment but said nothing about the dimension of fellowship. There is no authentic commitment to Christ apart from commitment to His people.

Perhaps this call to fellowship is for most of us the most threatening aspect of discipleship. We are afraid to love, to be loved, to get really close to other people. We fear that they will hurt us or laugh at us. As we come to know Christ, we know that we can trust Him, but we are suspicious of one another.

This was illustrated vividly by an incident which took place on New York's Lower East Side. While out walking with one of the residents there, I saw a beautiful Negro child bubbling with good humor and gaiety. As we passed, I smiled and said, "Hi." Immediately he smiled back and greeted me. "In a couple of years," my companion volunteered, "that little boy won't smile and say hi to a stranger. Living here, he learns that to be open to people is to be hurt, and soon he restrains his true feelings to protect himself."

What is true of people on the Lower East Side or in any ghetto is true of people everywhere, including those who live in suburbia. To protect ourselves, we hide our true feelings, our needs and our hopes, lest we be ridiculed.

But as the early disciples walked the countryside with our Lord, they must have learned how to become vulnerable to each other. Their actions, thoughts, motives, responses were all subject to the scrutiny and judgment of their peers. Perhaps their faith is demonstrated most vividly by their willingness to continue not only with Jesus but with one another. Authentic

Christianity in our day also requires that we be a part of a pilgrim fellowship who share life together.

III. *Commitment to Adventure*

Finally, the initial call to discipleship was a call to adventure. The early disciples were called to leave their families and the comfort and security of familiar ways and places, to go they knew not where, and to do they knew not what. Day by day they discovered that life was a great adventure, and that every hardship and every setback was a doorway to new service and maturity. Christ's call to His people, then and now, goes far beyond perfecting us, polishing us, or making us adequate. It is a call to follow Him into a life of involvement with people and into situations that would formerly have threatened us.

I once asked a charming and dynamic Christian woman in Alabama what was the biggest change that Christ had made in her. She replied that for the first thirty years of her life she had been haunted by a fear of failure. She had turned down all kinds of jobs and opportunities lest she fail. Yet today she is so filled with "holy boldness" that it is difficult to imagine her fearful of anything. This is the kind of change that Christ can bring about in His disciples.

Responding to the call does not always mean success in the world's terms. Two men I know, a plumbing contractor and a stockbroker, went bankrupt shortly after responding to Christ's call. But for each, "failure" led to a much wider ministry and a much deeper experience of life and service.

Recently I had lunch with a man who owns a chain of restaurants. He understands his particular call in terms of seeing his business as his parish, and all the people working for him as his spiritual and economic responsibility under God. He has become a person who is able to listen deeply to others, to ask questions, and to pray expectantly. Over lunch he recounted miracles in the lives of some of his employees who were "problem people" only a few weeks before. A new kind of team-work is developing in the heart of his flourishing busi-ness.

Some months ago my wife and I were doing a tele-vision show in a large eastern city. The announcer for the telecast had responded to the call of Christ some time before. He and his wife, partners in a mixed mar-riage and the victims of much misunderstanding, were reconciled as a result of their Christian commitment. But the most impressive thing to me was the number of people in that studio who had begun the Christian life or who had become intrigued by it because of the simple, dynamic love in this man. He was not an "evangelist," but simply an announcer living under new management, whose life was contagious to those around him. Surely this is the Great Adventure of our time for all of us, in our families, neighborhoods, jobs, and schools.

A couple in our town in New Jersey have meant much to my wife and me over the past years. George is a businessman and Florence an attractive, vivacious homemaker. Someone asked them, "What would you do if you knew you couldn't fail?" They talked about a ministry to lay leadership, and how much they would like to attempt such a ministry. After twenty years in the same business, George has left his job. He and his wife are now engaged in the ministry they had envisioned, and God is doing marvelous things through them.

A man on the West Coast once told me that his pre-school son had asked his mother, "Mommy, are we live or on tape?" This is a question that we should ask one another in the Church. Is life spontaneous or simply a dull, repetitive routine? The good news is that Jesus Christ is calling all who will hear to follow Him. The call is to a commitment to Him as Saviour, to His lordship over us, a commitment to fellowship with one another, and a commitment to adventure in every relationship and situation.

QUESTIONS FOR DISCUSSION

1. Describe a recent "serendipity" . . . that is, an unexpected blessing or benefit resulting from a rather ordinary encounter or circumstance.

2. When was the first time you became aware that God loved you?

3. If you could hear God say one thing to you, what do you think He would say?

4. If you knew God could hear you, what one thing would you most want to say to Him?

5. Where would you live if you could and what would you do there?

6. For what would you most like to be known in future history books, if your name were recorded for our time?

7. What would you do if you knew you couldn't fail?

7 | A New Look at the Priesthood

'TWAS THE WEEK before Christmas and all through the bus not a creature was stirring. We were packed in like sardines, with even standing room at a premium as regular commuters vied with last-minute shoppers for space. The road was slippery, traffic was heavy, and the bus was behind schedule. An atmosphere of irritation and gloom prevailed that was anything but a "holiday spirit."

I was standing near the center of the bus, facing sideways to catch the bit of light available for reading. In the seat just below me were two men wearing caps and leather jackets, who seemed somewhat out of place among the crowd of whitecollar workers. One was a man of middle years, the other a boy of twenty or so. I assumed that they were father and son. Just behind them were two nuns, chatting amiably and glancing from time to time at their open missals.

Suddenly the bus lurched to a stop and, caught off balance, I grabbed for a handhold to keep from falling. In doing so, I inadvertently struck a glancing blow to the head of the older man seated below. It must have felt like a karate chop!

Immediately I began to apologize and express my hope that he wasn't hurt, but he would not be placated. Instead, he denounced my carelessness in abusive language, especially for reading when I should have been holding on. My attempts to interrupt him and repeat my apology only enraged him further.

At this, the woman standing next to me got into the act. Indignant over the man's attitude, she let him know how difficult it was to be a standee.

"I paid for my seat!" he shouted.

"I paid for a seat, too!" she promptly replied.

At that he became more angry than ever. I fully expected him to get up and punch me in the nose. The young man with him tried to calm him down to no avail. Suddenly, with supreme sarcasm, another standee said, loud enough for the entire busload to hear: "Merry Christmas, Everybody!"

The grim greeting brought to an end the scene which had involved all those in the immediate area, who had been either listening intently, discussing it among themselves, or making loud comments. That is, everyone except the two nuns. They were busily reading their missals, looking neither right nor left.

At the first major stop, many people got off, including my angry "friend." To my immense satisfaction, he jostled someone in the aisle and had to make his own apologies.

The young man did not alight with his companion, and now that there were enough seats for all of us, I sat down beside him. As soon as I had settled myself, he smiled and said, "I hope you'll forgive him for the way he acted. You really picked the worst possible time to tangle with him. He's a bricklayer, and today he had an accident that almost cost him his hand. The foreman has threatened to fire him. Not only that, but he's having trouble with his wife, who's about to leave him."

"Is he a friend of yours?" I asked.

The boy shook his head. "I never saw him before. I'm a college student home for the holidays. We just happened to sit next to each other, and he told me his story as we rode along."

It occurred to me that we had lived through an incident typical of what happens in each of our lives many times a day. The setting may be an office, a home, a factory, a school, the board room in a plant, a church, or any of the backdrops against which we live out our lives. The circumstances may be different, but the cast of characters is the same. There are the offenders (the role I played in this case), the offended (the bricklayer coming home from work), the "sidetakers" (those who by words or attitudes defend or attack either of the antagonists), and lastly, the uninvolved (in this case, the two nuns).

But in the midst of this scene there was also a priest, a mediator — the young student who tried to bridge the gap between the bricklayer and me. He spoke first to the offended one, and later to the offender, trying to remove the barriers of misunderstanding.

We think of a priest as someone who mediates between man and God, and of Jesus Christ as our High Priest. But I would venture that no one can bring healing to human relationships without, to some degree, being an instrument of reconciliation to God.

There is an extaordinary statement in I Peter 2:9, 10: "But you are a chosen race, a royal priesthood, a holy nation, God's own people, that you may declare the wonderful deeds of him who called you out of darkness into his marvelous light. Once you were no people but now you are God's people; once you had not received mercy but now you have received mercy."

Who is called to be a priest? Everyone who is a Christian. To whom does the New Testament say, "You are a royal priesthood"? To *believers*. The moment you acknowledge the lordship of Christ in your life, you are qualified and commissioned to enter "the priesthood of all believers."

Renewal in the Church today depends upon every Christian's discovering that he is a priest, and then exercising his priesthood. This discovery has little to do with being a priest in ecclesiastical garb, entangled in church affairs. It has a great deal to do with being a priest for Christ in the secular world where most of us live and die day by day.

Where do you begin to be a priest? You begin where you are. It is not necessary to hurry home from work and then off to some special place to exercise the priesthood. We become priests in the places where we spend the major part of our day, earning a living or raising a family.

What can one do to be an effective priest in everyday life? Let me suggest three things:

(1) *Become involved with people and with life.* For many of us this is not easy. We fear rejection and ridicule and the hurt that comes with involvement. Hurt and misunderstanding are inevitable. Becoming involved means that we must live with people so that we understand their pain, pressure, tension, and fear. But the message of the Incarnation is that God dared to become involved with us in the person of His Son Jesus Christ. He entered into our circumstances, becoming one of us. He became vulnerable, setting an example that we are to follow.

Recently I met the youth minister of a large Baptist church in the Midwest. He is doing an outstanding job with young people in his town, but God has also called him to a ministry to older men — pensioners, drifters, the lonely, and the retired. As a consequence, he has moved to a room in the town's cheapest hotel, where a number of older men live.

I have visited his room and had coffee there with him and some of his new friends. The room is worn and shabby, and twenty-six people on that floor share one toilet. But this gifted young man understands that if he is to be a priest to some of the forgotten men in his town, he must share their lot and become involved in their lives.

(2) *Don't feel that you have to give answers.* An authentic priest is not a Mr. Fix-It. He may be an interpreter, or a bridge, but he is seldom an answer man. Sometimes the least helpful thing to do is to give someone an answer to his problem.

An executive in an insurance company in Newark,

New Jersey, was having problems. He had begun to drink too much; he had almost lost his job; his family life was disintegrating. Then he discovered the reality of Jesus Christ through the preaching and pastoral love of a faithful clergyman and through the warm, accepting fellowship of some ordinary people meeting in small groups.

Out of gratitude, he wanted to help others to find the life that he had found. Though he was no longer young, and had a large family to support, he felt a call to the ministry, and he interpreted this to mean that he should enroll in a theological seminary. His wife, however, could not see how he could provide for his family and go through the years of schooling necessary to become an ordained clergyman.

He discussed his problem with a friend, who questioned, "Why the ordained ministry?"

"Because I want to help people."

"Can you look around at people in your office and recognize some of the same needs that were yours a few years ago?" his friend asked.

"Of course," he replied, "When you've been there yourself, you know the signs."

"Then, perhaps, most of those people can be helped *best* by a fellow layman."

This opened a new door. The insurance man learned to identify with people and to let them know that he had not only suffered as they were suffering, but that he still had some of their temptations and problems. He loved people, listened to them, and found that Christ could use him as a lay priest.

(3) *Pray expectantly with and for people.* The businessman mentioned above learned that after loving

and listening, what was necessary was not *answers* but *prayer*. We pray secretly *for* people, and at the right moment we pray *with* them. Faith may be little more than expecting the impossible. When we begin to believe that no one is hopeless, and claim the fact that Jesus Christ is alive and able to perform miracles, we communicate our faith to others. God greatly uses this faith-attitude in His authentic priests. We believe *for people* that they can change.

Not long ago I talked with a courageous woman who has undergone a partial paralysis. In the early stages of her disease she was confined to a wheelchair. When at last she was able to leave the house, a friend took her to the supermarket to do some shopping. At the checkout counter, a hurrying customer bumped into her wheelchair as she waited in line.

Annoyed, he turned and said, "People like you don't belong in busy places like this. Why don't you stay home and keep out of the way?"

Those words sent my friend back to her apartment for another eighteen months of confinement. Crushed by the chance remark of an irritable stranger, she was robbed of a year and a half of active involvement in the world.

What tremendous power each of us has over the lives of others! We can help or destroy with a few words. Being a priest for Jesus Christ is simply using this influence in conscious or unconscious ways to help others break through the barriers that separate them from God or from other people. A growing "priesthood of believers" is a crucial aspect of God's strategy for renewal in our time.

QUESTIONS FOR DISCUSSION

1. Think of a person at your place of work, your school, or in your neighborhood who you feel is an authentic example of the lay priesthood (i.e.: a person who tries to be a bridge of understanding between God and man or between man and man or between groups). What characteristics make this person different from most other people?

2. Give a specific example from your own life of being helped in your relationship with God or with someone else by a lay "priest."

3. What single change in your own attitude would make you a more effective "priest" in your home, work, or neighborhood?

4. What do you find to be the worst pressures and strains in your work?

5. What do you find most boring and unenjoyable in your work?

6. What do you enjoy most in your work?

7. What are your special qualifications for your work?

8. How do you know your work is appreciated by others?

9. What are your ambitions and goals in your work?

8 | A New Look at Teaching

A NEW DIMENSION in teaching and learning is emerging in our time in the focus on the lay priesthood. If we affirm the New Testament and the Reformation belief that every Christian is called to be a priest, we get a fresh insight into the nature of the Church. The Church can no longer be a place where a few gifted preachers and teachers are the sole communicators of truth. If every man is a priest, every man is a discoverer and a participant with God, and he has something valid to report about God from his own experience. The Bible is the *corrective* for our experience, but the experience itself may be the initial source of information and the Bible its authentication.

Not long ago, in studying the material put out by one of our leading denominations for use in women's circles, I realized anew the need for the Church to understand the radical nature of the lay apostolate. As fresh and attractive as the printed material seemed to be, its underlying basis was that of an author instructing women and asking questions designed to get them to discuss what he was trying to say. How important it is for the Church to trust its lay people themselves to discover relevant, contemporary truths from God! The questions in our circle studies — and men's studies and young people's studies — must not be questions that merely encourage the participants to grapple with the author's teaching. Rather, they should be questions which make the participants grapple with their own understanding of God's will for them and for the world, from experiences and insights gained in their own daily lives.

Certainly there is a sense in which God has ordained a few to be preachers and teachers, experts on principle and theory and exegesis and exposition of the Bible. But all Christians can become experimenters with Him in daily life and can then report their discoveries.

In this way, we find that new Christians can sometimes teach seasoned veterans, and young Christians can teach the old. There is no hierarchy in this arrangement. Every Christian is launched on a life of experiment, discovery, and faith from which he can report on new ways that God may be working in specific situations.

The key to this approach to learning is the answer to the question, "Is God teaching through just a few,

or is every Christian a potential channel of truth?"
Communications expert Marshall McLuhan says that
we are living in an age in which we are experiencing
the "participation mystique." This truth from a secular
source underscores the reality that every Christian is
potentially a teacher of every other Christian.

Let me cite several examples of how this insight may
unlock and release learning and participation on a vast
new scale.

From time to time I find myself leading a workshop
at a conference. A workshop permits conferees to sort
themselves out according to interest. They meet for an
hour or so to explore a certain topic. On many such
occasions, I have seen some startling truths come, not
from expert teachers and preachers, but from the rank
and file of Christians.

Once in Los Angeles I was assigned to a workshop
entitled, "How To Love the Unlovely." Almost a hundred people were in attendance. I began by explaining
something of what I have stated here and suggesting
an experiment. My "teaching" consisted of asking only
two questions. After suggesting that all of us had
certainly been "unlovely" from time to time — which
everyone affirmed — I asked: "Who loved you when
you were the most unlovely?" There was a response
from nearly every person in that room. Each one could
name a person who had been an incarnation of God's
love for him when he had been at his worst.

My second question was: "What did this person do
or say that communicated God's love to you? What
primary attitude did he demonstrate?" Again, after
some thought, people responded with brief, clinical
reports on what incarnate love looks like. We listed

these qualities on the blackboard and God gave us the most astonishing picture of "love on two legs." Lovers of the unlovely were characterized like this: "He accepted me as I was"; "He didn't feel superior"; "She believed I could change"; "He spent time with me"; and "She cared about how I felt."

At a recent conference in Phoenix I was asked to lead a workshop on "Healing Broken Relationships." Again, attendance reflected people's interest in life-centered topics, and everyone in the room admitted that at some time he had been a part of a broken relationship. Some, in fact, were still experiencing painful alienation. Again I asked two questions. My first question was: "What was the first thing you or the other person did which indicated that the relationship was breaking?" Almost everyone had something to contribute. Some people mentioned second or third causes or reactions, but many were able to remember the root causes of a break.

As specific causes were named, we could see that two of the primary things which break a relationship are our great need for love and the fear that we will be rejected by the other. With this combination of need and fear, we see how a relationship is broken if one person feels slighted. Discovering these root causes was an important learning experience for us all in understanding human nature.

My second question was: "If this relationship has been healed by God, what is the first thing you or the other person did to initiate His healing?" Here we received a long list of lessons out of people's lives; not only such obvious things as having to apologize or "go the second mile," but more subtle and elusive insights. There was not one of us in that workshop who didn't learn a great deal from God about the nature of sin and the appropriation of God's grace in relationships through the shared experience of the group.

A third workshop in which I recently took part was entitled, "How To Help People." This produced a learning situation similar to that which grew out of "loving the unlovely."

First, I asked: "What single person has been of greatest help to you in terms of discovering wholeness and authenticity in Christ?" The second followed: "What did this person *do* to channel God's transforming power to your life?" People mentioned such things as: "She listened to me"; "He was honest about himself"; "He did not feel superior"; "He always had time for me"; "He wanted to know what I was thinking and feeling, and it seemed important to him"; and "She believed that I could do a great deal more than I was now doing."

This past year we have experimented with a number of clergy conferences across the land, focused on renewal in the Church. Exciting times have resulted when we have dared in small groups and workshops to ask the following questions: "What single activity in the Church has been most meaningful to you in terms of personal growth and healing?" It has been surprising to hear clergymen mention the kinds of relationships and primary groups that God has used to help, heal, and transform them.

"Is this the kind of program you are now emphasizing in your own church?" The answer to this has been an overwhelming "No." Clergymen often push programs that are handed down "from above," not daring to believe that they should put primary stress on the things that God has already used in their own lives.

Through the learning situation created in these clergy conferences, we have dared to affirm that God has shown us valid ways and means for personal renewal. Now we, as clergy, need to offer these ways and means to other people. When this happens, there will be widespread renewal in the Church.

I believe that there is almost no area of practical human concern that cannot be approached in this way. When Sunday school classes, communicants' classes, and groups of inquirers get together to discover how to be effective in any area, an entirely new way of drawing on God's wisdom and knowledge will be discovered.

QUESTIONS FOR DISCUSSION

1. Describe the most effective teacher you ever had and tell what you think there was about his manner or method that made him effective.

2. Describe the class or small group which you feel contributed most to your understanding and application of the Christian life.

3. Analyze the uniqueness of that group and its leadership.

4. What "life situation problem" from the chapter would you like to consider in your group? For example, you might take: "How does God heal broken relationships?"

    (a) What was the *first* thing you or the other person *did* which indicated that the relationship was breaking?

    (b) What do the answers to (a) indicate about the nature of relationships in general?

    (c) If this relationship has been healed, what is the *first* thing you or the other person did to initiate healing?

5. Make up your own questions for another life-situation problem to use in your group.

9 | A New Look at Wholeness

SEVERAL YEARS AGO a Canadian woman went to a conference where she was challenged to begin the Christian life. When she accepted this challenge her personality changed remarkably. She later reported that for years in her office she had been referred to — behind her back — as "the old bag." But only a few days after she had committed her life to God, the same office colleagues began to address her, "Hey, Kid!"

Although she may not have influenced her co-workers to duplicate her spiritual step, they could nevertheless recognize and appreciate the wholeness that had come to her.

In studying the Bible we discover, to our fascination, that the salvation Jesus came to bring is expressed in the word *sozo*, which means to save "in the religious sense of salvation and in the sense of healing a disease." The very name "Saviour" means healer. The Bible constantly implies that there is a connection between health (of mind and body) and salvation, or between sickness and sin. Jesus as the Messiah was the bringer of "health and salvation." The Christian picture of Jesus as the Great Physician, the Saviour of both the body and the soul, is founded on all the stories in the gospels. Jesus Himself said, "They that are whole have no need of a physician, but they that are sick."

The closing verses in the fifth chapter of James indicate the radical nature of this salvation. Here the physical, emotional, and spiritual are all interwoven in the concept of salvation.

Spiritual wholeness ought to be discernible to the secular world. When Jesus cleansed a leper or healed the demoniac of Gadara, He sent each back to his world for confirmation of his wholeness.

God is truth and truth is one in every discipline — medical, scientific, and philosophical. Two chemists working side by side in a laboratory, one a Christian and one a non-Christian, may differ in motivation, attitudes, and integrity, but in chemistry they share the same goals and methods. This is obviously true in the practice of medicine. A Christian doctor and a non-Christian doctor, attending the same patient, share the same medical and therapeutic resources and hope for the same physical results. If the patient experiences healing — through medicine, therapy, or prayer — both doctors will recognize it. The only obvious difference between the doctors is that one identifies Christ as the source of life and truth and healing.

Jesus said, "I came that they might have life. . . ." This life He brings is wholeness which certainly encompasses emotions, relationships, and attitudes. If Christian conversion does not begin a process of wholeness in these areas, discernible to friends and colleagues as well as to any medical or psychiatric specialist who may be observing, something is wrong. If our attitudes and relationships are not improved, we are not experiencing the wholeness that Christ came to bring.

Jesus Himself was the only completely whole person who ever lived. However, a secular historian said of the early Christians that they out-lived, out-loved, and out-died their pagan contemporaries. The world may not appreciate the Healer, but it sees and appreciates the authentic healing He brings to His disciples.

While listening recently to a professor of psychiatry from Harvard, I was struck with the similarity between the wholeness Christ offers and the wholeness which is the goal of modern psychiatry. The doctor outlined four components of mental health that would be acceptable to almost every psychiatrist today, whatever his training or approach.

(1) *"The capacity to love another."* It's easy for most of us to love humanity. It's the person we live with whom we can't stand! Psychiatry differentiates between a generalized love and the capacity to sustain a deep relationship with one other person. Unless we are capable of the latter, we cannot meet the requirements of mental health or the requirements of our Lord. Jesus said, "How can you love God whom you

have not seen, if you cannot love your brother whom you have seen?"

(2) *"A sound, consistent conscience with well-defined precepts."* Neither Christianity nor psychiatry makes perfection a hallmark of wholeness. Rather, wholeness is awareness of wrong, combined with the implied desire to make amends. Reading the New Testament convinces me that the early Christians were not made perfect by their faith. Rather, they received the Holy Spirit to guide and reprimand them when they missed the mark. The sick person (Christian or non-Christian) either does not know right from wrong or he must justify his every action. Eric Berne, psychiatrist and author of *Games People Play*, says that his criterion for emotional and mental health is an individual's ability to say, "Yes," "No," and "Whoopee!" The emotionally ill say, "Yes, but. . . ." "No, but. . . ." and they are unable to say, "Whoopee!"

(3) *"A strong sense of identity."* One of the neurotic symptoms of our time is that people apparently tend more and more to be "other-directed." We take our cues for behavior, attitudes, and goals from those around us, and these vary from group to group. Mental health requires that we be the same person in every group. In the Christian context, we see the early Christians, whether carried on the shoulders of an adoring crowd or shipwrecked or in dungeons, maintaining their individuality, integrity, and identity as children of God and ambassadors of Christ. They transformed their environment rather than simply reflecting it.

A modern illustration is the Christian martyr, Dietrich Bonhoeffer, whose Nazi jailers were continually replaced because of his influence on them, even as with the Apostle Paul during his imprisonment in Rome.

(4) *"To come to terms with the fact of your own death."* Psychiatrists tell us that the fear of death is increasingly producing a breakdown of life. But while they diagnose this condition, what can they do to alleviate it? What can man say to man about the ultimate fact, death? The great dynamic of Christianity is the fact that Jesus Christ has broken the hold of death on man by His own death and resurrection. The Christian is free to live extravagantly and sacrificially because he is not afraid to die. In the words of the Apostle Paul, "For me to live is Christ and to die is gain."

The shape of wholeness for the Christian and for all men must be the same. We see Jesus Christ as the unique author and enabler of the wholeness sought by men everywhere. But, whatever degree of wholeness the Christian has received, he is responsible for using it not to serve his own ends but to serve God's purposes for the world.

QUESTIONS FOR DISCUSSION

1. Tell who you are, apart from your titles, honors, or job description.

2. What is your most satisfying single accomplishment: before you were 6? between the ages of 6 and 12? 12 and 18? 18 and 25? over 25?

3. If you had what you really wanted in life, what would you have?

4. What would you *most* like to do or be for the next five years if there were no limitations (of family, money, education, health, age, etc.)?

5. Describe the last time you remember being criticized and analyze your reactions to that criticism.

6. As you think over the significant decisions of your life, what percentage do you think resulted from your own choice and what percentage came about through external circumstances? Give an example of each.

10 | A New Look at Healing

In DOZENS OF CLERGY conferences across the continent during the past two years, I have seen how irrelevant doctrinal issues have become, and how relevant are the issues of communicable life as compared to meaningless forms and practices. Jesus said He came that we might have life! He never said that He came to make us "religious." Today both laymen and clergymen are eager to discover this authentic life which comes from Christ and which is both transforming and communicable to man in his multiple needs.

Some years ago when I was beginning my ministry as a clergyman, I was puzzled by the success local chapters of Alcoholics Anonymous had with people whom I had been unable to help. Because I was threatened, I compared my doctrinal position with the doctrinal position of those who were most effective in AA work. Often these people were, in my opinion, either "doctrinally unsound" or not professing Christians at all — yet their methods were successful.

Some years later, while doing graduate study in the field of psychology, I made a discovery that shed much light on my former confusion. A University of Chicago doctrinal candidate had done a study involving tape recordings of a great many psychiatrists at work. Some of them were leaders of their own schools of psychiatry; others were their disciples.

Unlabeled tape recordings were played to people working in the field, who were asked to classify the people they heard according to their schools of thought. Most of the listeners thought that the leaders of the *various* psychiatric schools were members of the *same* school. In other words, the ablest and most gifted men in the field of personal counseling sounded pretty much alike when they were actually working with patients.

If you asked one of those outstanding therapists what made him effective as a counselor, and made him presume to write books and train others in the field, he would probably stress his theories of personality and his particular clinical approach. But in fact, the test indicated that these theories of personality and methods of approach seemed to be relatively unimportant. The therapist *was* something and *did* something to others of which he may have been quite unaware.

To me this was fascinating. Psychology at that time had fallen into the same kind of rut in which the Church often finds itself. Since then we have come to see that doctrinal views or clinical views are not enough in dealing with the needs of individuals. There are things that we do and say and embody that *are* important, but they are *not* theoretical. If the Church of Jesus Christ is to rediscover its relevance, it will be as we find what we can say and do that will let God bring His wholeness through us to others.

Let me state the problem in another way. Imagine two churches where the pastors and people have theological views which are almost identical. Yet in one church people are finding forgiveness, fellowship, and relevant service and beginning to live as Jesus Christ intends them to live. In the other church people seem separated, relationships are superficial, and nothing that remotely resembles "good news" is being experienced.

Or think of two other churches in the same town with totally different theological views and ecclesiastical approaches. One may be a high church, the other a very low church; one conservative and the other liberal. But in *both* churches, a person in deep trouble can find the help and the power of the living Christ to begin life anew.

What I am suggesting is that there is a shape of healing that is discernible and that can be identified clinically today and scripturally in the New Testament. If we know what to look for, we will find that two churches that seem to be very different may not actually be so dissimilar. What are the "active ingredients" in local churches and groups where people are finding health, wholeness, and life?

New York City, where Faith at Work has its offices, has a serious drug problem. Hundreds of groups of all kinds are attempting to work with dope addicts, but most of them honestly admit that they have no long-term success.

However, there are three groups that seem to have a remarkable success with addicts — and apparently a lasting one. These three groups are totally dissimilar to one another in doctrine. One is a Christian group; its orientation is Pentecostal and fundamentalistic. The second group is almost wholly psychological in its approach. The third group is explicitly *non*-spiritual and *non*-psychological.

If you were to ask those at the center of leadership in these three groups what it is that makes their group successful, you would get predictable answers. One would say that it is the power of the Holy Spirit. Another would say that it is applying the most relevant forms of psychotherapy. The third would talk about a communal kind of living that is far superior to anything psychological or Christian.

A study of these three diverse groups reveals that they have four things in common — things which are relevant to human beings in all conditions, not simply dope addicts. Any church attempting to minister effectively to its people, whatever their "insoluble problems," must incorporate at least these four ingredients:

(1) *Possibility of Change*. Each group preaches a gospel that says it is possible for a man to change. They may give different reasons for this change, or they may attribute change to different internal or external drives or forces, but they are alike in that they give hope to the hopeless. Most of us know that both psychiatry and some in the Church have become very skeptical of helping true drug addicts. It seems presumptuous to suggest that a man can change, and

change quite radically and suddenly. But on the basis of their experience, these three groups hold out this very hope. As Christians we can see that this is the crux of the good news in Jesus Christ. Man does not have to be what he is. Because God entered the world in Jesus Christ, no man is hopeless and no man has to remain unchanged.

(2) *New Values.* Each of these groups believes that it is possible for man to develop a new set of values and goals to live by. Again, this approach is unpopular both in psychology and in religion. We are too sophisticated to think that after a lifetime of holding false values a man can suddenly develop responsibility and higher ethics and, in effect, find a new conscience. But all three of these groups dare to challenge people to accept new values and to live by them. What is more, they *expect* people to do this — and their expectation is often fulfilled. Each group can point to "walking miracles," totally different from the men and women who came into that group some years back.

We can appreciate that these three groups have stumbled onto something which is basic to the Christian life. As Christians, we believe that the Holy Spirit can enter a man and give him new standards to live by. In point of fact, he can have a new conscience. If we do not expect people to change in terms of goals and standards, we minimize the tremendous miracles that God is able to perform in them.

(3) *A Fellowship of Like Sufferers.* The three groups see as basic to a person's discovering wholeness that he needs to belong to a fellowship of like sufferers. Those who are receiving help meet together in small

groups to talk about common problems and to rejoice in common victories. Of course this is also the genius of Alcoholics Anonymous. But we must discover in the Church that this kind of fellowship of like sufferers is at the very heart of the Christian enterprise as God intends it. There can be no renewal in a local church until its members come together according to their particular needs to share defeats, rejoice in victories, and sustain and affirm one another in the day-by-day living-out of life in Christ.

(4) *Ministry to Others.* Alcoholics Anonymous is famous for its twelfth-step work, whereby those who have begun to find sobriety immediately begin to help others who are looking for sobriety. In just this way the three groups we have been discussing send their people out to work actively with other dope addicts, bearing witness to the fact that individuals can change and offering to help others to discover a life free from drugs.

Apathy and deadness in the Church today are the result of the failure of Christians to understand that evangelism and person-to-person ministry are a must, not just for the world's sake but for the sake of the individual Christian. People need our help, but even more do we need to be those who are constantly transmitting and channeling life and help in relevant ways to others.

As I travel across the country, visiting churches of all kinds, sizes, shapes, and doctrinal positions, I find that those where life is welling up and being channeled to others are churches that have discovered these four ingredients that make up the shape of healing. Renewal comes to a church where both the pulpit and the pew by preaching and witness challenge men to change, enable them to find and live by new values, offer a fellowship of sufferers to all who are lonely, and urge and encourage one another to find a ministry in the world.

QUESTIONS FOR DISCUSSION

1. Was there a recent problem in your life which seemed to be insoluble? What was it?

2. If you discovered total or partial help for your "insoluble" problem, describe the means by which it came to you. If you did not find help, describe the resources you relied upon and analyze why you think they failed.

3. What things make or keep your life complicated?

4. List the things that you do to keep your life simple.

5. What *could* you do to make your life simpler?

6. What are your personal long-range goals? short-range goals?

7. Tell how you help or hinder those you live or work with in attaining their personal goals.

11 | A New Look at Relationships

ABOUT SIX MONTHS ago I met a delightful married couple whom I have come to think of as a modern Priscilla and Aquilla. We have spent a good deal of time together, enough so that we know each other intimately. Not long ago they came into my office, closed the door, and said, "Bruce, we want to talk to you. Don't say anything. Just listen until we have finished."

Then for the next half hour they told me what they thought of me. They began by saying that they were aware of my shortcomings, sins, lacks, and weaknesses, but they felt that I also knew these weak points. What I didn't know, they said, was the uniqueness of my gifts, assets, and strong points. In an affirmative and appreciative way, they began to list the strengths and skills and gifts and characteristics they had observed in me.

When they had finished, we had prayer together and my whole life and direction and ministry were once again offered to God. But this time I could offer Him with assurance the strengths He had given me, not just my many sins and shortcomings.

Since that day, my colleagues and friends and family have seen a change in me and have commented on the new authority and self-acceptance which are coming to me. For one thing, I can be honest with people about what they are — both the positive and negative aspects — because I now see myself in the positive as well as in the negative.

In trying to understand what God has begun in my life through the unique ministry of these two friends, I have thought a lot about our Lord's ministry to individuals as reported in the four gospels. Jesus spent a great deal of time alone with individuals. We are all aware that they came away from those encounters with Him transformed and liberated.

First of all, and perhaps the most dramatic example, are the twelve disciples. By calling these ordinary men to follow Him and to become fishers of men and to build a new kingdom, He was affirming their present strengths and believing in their potential abilities.

His attitude toward the Samaritan prostitute by the well indicates that He saw not only what she was but what she could be. His sensitive questioning of the demoniac in Gadara shows the same thing. His treatment of Zacchaeus, the leader from the political establishment, and Nicodemus, the leader from the religious establishment, also indicates a ministry of affirmation to people who were caught in their peculiar frustrations and brokenness.

Again, with the woman taken in adultery, His gentleness and sensitivity reveal an affirmation of her true self and of what she could be if she believed in her own strengths and put them at God's disposal.

The list could go on and on. The gospels are full of stories of individuals made new and different because of an encounter with Jesus Christ. By word and action and attitude, He communicated to people that they were important and that they had something to offer to God.

Perhaps the one word that best sums up Jesus' personal ministry is *affirmation*. People began to respond to Him long before they were fully aware of His teaching. And though the Cross is the most important single event in human history, Jesus was able to communicate the love of God long before the event of His death and resurrection.

In the light of my own experience with the contemporary Priscilla and Aquilla, I have tried to think of possible attitudes we can adopt toward people we meet. It seems to me that there are only four possibilities — and, of course, an infinite variety of combinations of the four.

(1) *Indifference.* In today's jargon this might be termed "playing it cool." But whatever form indifference takes, it is the opposite of love, and always destructive. When we are with someone who is indifferent to us, be it a husband or wife or parent or child, a colleague, a competitor, or even a stranger, we feel minimized and of little worth.

(2) *Flattery*. Like indifference, flattery is always harmful and never constructive. It is nothing more or less than manipulation. It is the adult form of a baby's crying and demanding his own way. It is the ultimate in sophisticated self-centeredness. The things we tell people are aimed at getting them to respond in a way that will be helpful to us.

(3) *Criticism*. Though criticism is usually harmful, and, I suspect, comes most often from wrong motives, it can be helpful at times. When people begin to move in the direction of love, they see that they must forego indifference and flattery, and they often begin to criticize the people they care about. All of us need criticism sometimes. As has been said, "Faithful are the wounds of a friend." Most of us suffer from a lack of criticism from faithful friends. But although criticism is often necessary and sometimes helpful, it is not the best method of bringing about a changed life.

(4) *Affirmation*. Affirmation, which is quite different from flattery, is almost always helpful. It is the process of putting our faith into words, and telling people positive truths about themselves. Many of us are "dying" for lack of a word of affirmation!

We may be suspicious of affirmation because it looks and sounds like flattery, which we know to be destructive. But the basic difference between flattery and affirmation is that affirmation deals in truths, whereas flattery deals in lies or half-truths, or truths for the wrong reason.

Recently I have come across some powerful examples of what happens to people as the result of this kind of affirmation. Some months ago I met General Bruce Medaris, a remarkable person who for many years held a key position in America's space program. A life-long churchman, General Medaris has recently had a pro-found conversion and has discovered the power of the living Christ to heal his body and to change his life and attitudes.

In talking to him, I discovered that the turning point in General Medaris's life came many years before his conversion. He describes himself as having been a very self-sufficient, determined man. During World War II, when he was serving on General Omar Bradley's staff, he was forced to take a position in a staff meeting concerning the allied invasion of Europe that would profoundly affect an important tactical decision that General Bradley was about to make.

When Bruce Medaris had had his say, General Brad-ley asked if he knew what this change in plans would involve. Having been assured that Medaris realized what effect his judgment would have, Bradley said, "Very well, the plans will be changed. As long as you are my ordnance officer, your professional judgment will be followed. When I no longer believe you're the best man to handle ordnance, somebody else will have your job."

Bruce Medaris says that it was the first time in his life that anyone had trusted him to that extent. As a result, he no longer had to fight. Someone believed in him, trusted him, and accepted his judgment. This clear-cut affirmation changed his life.

Most of us who have been fighting for a place in the sun need to hear some fellow human being speak a word of affirmation. Who knows but that this word may come from God Himself? We all have the power to affect the lives of those around us. What a wise man General Bradley must have been, to treat his staff in a way that brought about not only victory in Europe but also the transformation of people.

Here is another example of the power of affirmation. For the past few years I have known a gifted young man who won a writers' contest in Wisconsin and who now has been given a full scholarship to a great university.

The story behind the story is that my friend Joe was a terrible student and a high school drop-out. He became involved in crime, and was sentenced to a twenty-year prison term for armed robbery. In prison, he began to borrow books from the chaplain's library. They were difficult, complex books, and the chaplain asked Joe if he understood them. Joe said he did.

After further questioning about the content of the books, the chaplain said that Joe must be brilliant. Joe said no, he was stupid and had had a terrible time in school.

It turned out that all his life Joe had been told he was stupid, and he believed it. But with a word of affirmation from the chaplain, he began to believe that God had given him not only a marvelous mind but also great perception and sensitivity. He began to read more and more, and to try his hand at writing stories. Now he is exploring his God-given abilities, developing his skills, and thinking about how he can use them to help others. Apart from the word of affirmation from a chaplain in a penitentiary, Joe might have gone through life being "stupid."

A more homely illustration comes from my own family. Just now our fifth-grader is starting to blossom as a student. He's far from the best student in his class, but he has moved up several notches and is no longer at the bottom.

This happy change was precipitated by Mark's present teacher. When I met her I discovered that she happens to like boys who aren't always attentive, who may be poor spellers and sloppy in their work. What a remarkable gift this teacher has! Instead of perpetually criticizing, she affirms strengths that are there. The result in our Mark is a desire to produce better work. I thank God for all such teachers who can refrain from making well-deserved criticisms and can sprinkle in some basic affirmation by words and attitudes.

Finally, let me suggest that this ministry of affirmation can work wonders in a marriage. I talked to a woman who described her marriage, and it certainly sounded like a stalemate. For years she and her husband had had almost no verbal or physical communication. Their evenings together were spent in sitting and watching television. The wife was lonely beyond words. She confided in me that she loved her husband, but was not sure that he still loved her.

I suggested to her that as an act of faith she might one day put on her prettiest dress and some French perfume and, in the middle of a television show, sit down on her husband's lap and tell him that he was wonderful.

She was appalled at the suggestion. "What is the worst thing that could happen?" I asked. "He might laugh," she said, after considering it for a moment.

"That's true," I said, "but are you willing to risk it to find out what his response might be?"

A week later the wife wrote me an ecstatic letter. "Guess what!" it began. "I tried what you suggested — and he didn't laugh!"

Here is an example of two people in a stalemate, in which each is afraid to affirm the other lest he be laughed at. In faith we may have to break the stale-mate by deep affirmation. Certainly it won't always work, but the fact that it will sometimes work makes it well worth trying.

We Christians are accustomed to practicing the ministry of exhortation, which comes in many forms. But exhortation is really urging someone to be better than he is, or to perform more adequately than he has in the past. Paul Tillich gives us a word of caution. "Don't say the demanding 'be' to anybody without fear and hesitation, for this word 'be' contains in its two letters the whole riddle of the relation of man to God. You may destroy a life by demanding something of a person that he is not!"*

What a wise word from a great thinker! There is a place for exhortation, but all too often it implies that you find someone inadequate and urge him to become something which he suspects he is not.

By contrast, affirmation includes appreciation for what the person already is and for the qualities God has built into his life. While exhortation is sometimes helpful, affirmation can bring about the liberation and release of a human personality.

Sin is real and must be dealt with. The cross of Jesus Christ attests to the reality of sin and the terrible price God has paid to deal with our rebelliousness and unbelief. But if, in a relationship with a person, we begin with affirmation, we may find that he is then free in a new way to confess his sin and to repent. When we begin with exhortation or confrontation, he

---

*From *The Courage to Be,* by Paul Tillich. Quoted by permission of the Yale University Press.

may be so threatened that he cannot face the real nature of sin.

The example of our Lord in His dealings with individuals seems to me to involve a liberating ministry of affirmation. The cross says that God loves us. Can we not then love each other, and express this in our words and attitudes?

As our Lord encountered people we see how He delighted in them, loved them, believed in them, enjoyed them. The cross is always in the background as the ultimate mark of love. But in Jesus Christ there is also a word of affirmation and encouragement. We hear Him commanding us to "love one another as I have loved you," urging us to use the keys of the Kingdom to unlock the mystery of personality.

The Gospel is good news. We have a terrible and wonderful commission to live out the Gospel, and to proclaim that in Jesus Christ God is for man. Because He is for people, we are for people.

QUESTIONS FOR DISCUSSION

1. Who was the first person in your life who you thought really "understood" you?

2. What was that person like?

3. Describe his (her) effect on you.

4. List what you think are your three best characteristics . . . then your three worst characteristics.

5. Tell each member of your group what you most admire about him or her.

12 | The Need for Authentic Heroes

To BE SOMEBODY'S HERO is a humbling experience. Every athletic star, every topflight business executive, every minister, youth worker, and schoolteacher knows that it is both thrilling and disquieting to be a "knight in shining armor" to one or two or a dozen or a multitude of people. Yet I think there is a sense in which every Christian should be a hero, at least to a few people. The Bible speaks of Christians being the light of the world and if we walk in the light we can't avoid being seen.

Paul the Apostle said to the churchmen in Thessalonica, "You became our followers and the Lord's . . .

then you yourselves became an example." Being Exhibit A to the ancient Greeks did not seem to frighten Paul, who even said to King Agrippa, "I wish that you were just like me. . . ." Yet he was wise enough to know that he and his friends could not hide the "cracks in their armor."

Have you ever been embarrassed by the Bible's candid description of the private lives of the heroes of the faith? Abraham was a liar, Jacob was a cheat, Moses was a coward, and David an adulterer. Yet these are the examples given in the book of Hebrews in the marvelous chapter on heroes of the faith.

Being a hero implies leadership, virtue, strength, but it does *not* imply perfection. A legitimate hero acknowledges his weakness as well as his strength.

Many Christians say, by indirection, "I used to be a terrible person. Then I met Jesus. Now I don't have any problems." If, by silence, you don't let people know where you are still struggling and hurting, you betray them.

An authentic hero should project a full image. When you show only your virtues, your victories — and by great self-effort exhibit an unflawed image (which is only a half-image), you mislead people. You cheat them. You contribute to the feeling of guilt inside them.

What happens is this: they try to be like you. Now knowing that the pressures they feel are common to you, too, they feel, "I'm no good, I can't make it. I'm full of doubt and resentment and fear. I've failed." They turn back from the experiment of faith, thinking that they are not virtuous enough.

Paul tells us that we have a treasure, but in an earthen vessel. We must speak about the treasure, but we must also say unashamedly, "Look at the earthen vessel. I still argue with my wife. I'm touchy. I get hurt, and sometimes I sulk. I often have a bad temper. I'm getting better, I think, but the problem is still there. Help me with it."

In the Bible the lives of the great men of God are turned inside out to show us their inner battles, their weaknesses, their revolts against heaven. The Bible is a history of conflict, of human tensions, of assertion and submission, rebellion and obedience, defiance and reconciliation. God loves those who fight to defend themselves, who struggle, who don't give in easily. Today's heroes of the faith walk in the company of God's men through the ages: Samuel, Isaiah, Jeremiah, Peter, Paul, St. Augustine, Luther, Wesley — and now you.

In the name of Christ we have an obligation to bring to others our own humanity. We have to learn to say to our children and to the young people in our churches, classrooms, and activity groups: "I'm a cracked pot, an old earthen vessel, a hero with feet of clay! What a sense of humor God must have that He has chosen us to be His people. Isn't this good news!"

Let us hope that the generation we are attempting to lead will find in us disarming honesty rather than presumption or hypocrisy.

If we really believe that we are justified by faith in Jesus Christ, whom do we fear? And if I don't fear you, I am free to be transparent. I can let you see my weakness, and even relax in your presence. When we are justified by God we are free — free to fail, free to get angry, free to live. Jesus Christ came to make you and me free to be wholly man and woman. That means whole: intellectually, spiritually, socially, sexually.

How amazing that no matter how much He succeeds

in changing us over the decades and the millennia to come, He won't love us a bit more in the future than He loves us now. In the growing assurance of this love we can move out in the midst of our problems and live in the open — with abandon.

This does not mean that we are free to be immoral or irresponsible. It means to live fully within the bounds of responsibility. It means wrestling with that responsibility. God offers us a spontaneous morality — you are free to be your "cracked-pot" self, real, vivid, with royal rights for others.

Often Christians are reluctant to tell others about their faith or their Christian commitment, fearful that they will henceforth be figuratively wearing a sign that says, "Be like me!"

I believe we can say to the world, "Look. I'm not better than you are. It isn't my goodness or my knowledge of God that counts; but I can tell you about a relationship with Jesus Christ." This is a revolutionary thing.

QUESTIONS FOR DISCUSSION

1. What single person (other than spouse, parents, or children) has been the most influential in your life?

2. State a specific change in your own performance or attitudes that has come from your contact with that person.

3. What were the unique personality traits or characteristics in that person that account for his (her) impact on your life?

4. What groups, persons, or outside resources do you think contributed to this person's being what he is?

5. Since each of us is a "hero" to someone, describe specifically how you think you affect those who look up to you.